Hairy Knees *and* Heather Hills

Hairy *and* Knees
Heather Hills

Poems old and new from
Walter McCorrisken
(semi-skilled poet)

Birlinn

First published in Great Britain, in 1995,
by Birlinn Ltd,
13 Roseneath Street,
Edinburgh

British Library Cataloguing-in-Publication Data
A Catalogue record for this book is available from the
British Library.

ISBN: 1 874744 34 3

Designed And Typeset By Earlybird
Cover And Text Illustrated By John Gahagan

Printed and Bound in Finland
by Werner Söderström OY

CONTENTS

INTRODUCTION   7

1. ANIMALS   9

2. EPITAPHS TO PET DOGS   19

3. EPITAPHS TO PEOPLE   25

4. PEOPLE   35

5. LIMERICKS   51

6. ODDS AND ENDS   57

7. SLIGHTLY LONGER POEMS   75

8. MORE EPITAPHS   111

9. MORE ODDS AND ENDS   117

SEMI-SKILLED POET

Where is the poet of yesterday,
Who walked with heavy tread?
Ignoring the voice at midnight,
"For God's sake come to bed!"

Where is the poet of yesterday.
Who twisted the tortured word?
Who paced the floor till morning light
But nothing great occurred?

Where is the poet of yesterday,
Who sat with aching head?
Trying so hard to complete a line
And wishing that he were dead?

Where is the poet of yesterday,
With noble head and studied pose?
He sits in thought throughout the night
With cobwebs on his nose.

He's still sits there in deep despair,
Wearing his faither's jaicket,
He's realised he's semi-skilled
And never gonnae make it.

One

ANIMALS

THE HIPPO

Beauty is skin deep,
So they say.
So for the hippo,
Let us pray.

THE HUMBLE DOG

The humble dog
Is man's most grateful beast.
For a bone to us
Is to him a feast.

Dogs delight to sniff around
Little objects on the ground.
Yet scented ladies, why God knows,
Kiss these animals on the nose.

That's why these ladies,
Some call them crumpet,
Only get kissed upon the trumpet.

THE HORSE

A horse came galloping through the trees,
An animal in trepidation,
It caught its heid on a sycamore branch -
Suspended animation.

HIGHLAND BULL

Pity the hairy, Highland Bull,
As through this life he goes,
Because he has no fingers,
He wears a ring upon his nose.

A THREE-LEGGED DOG

A three-legged dog rode westward one day
Down to the jail at Moosejaw,
"Sheriff," he said on unsteady leg,
"Sheriff, Ah've come for ma paw."

THE HERON

"Have you got a cold?" said a heron
To another he met in a moat.
"Naw," said the other big heron,
"It's just a frog in ma throat."

HOME

An auld carpet to lie on
And maybe a bone.
It's no' much to us,
But to a dog it's a home.

BITCHES

Some women are called bitches
And other coarse names,
But the wee female dug,
Looks efter its weans.

DEFUNCT

If a' the animals
That are now defunct
Had no' been buried
They would have stunk.

THE PUDDOCK

The puddock loups quite happily,
Fae stane tae mossy stane,
And when he reaches the other bank
Loups happily back again.

A TINY DOG

A bus one day lost in a fog
Collided with a tiny dog
But oh, what damage could entail
If that wee dog had been a whale.

AN OLD TEDDY BEAR

Flowing gently on the tide
Strands of golden hair.
Shivering sadly by the fire
A balding Teddy Bear.

THE MOLE

"Onward, onward!" cried the mole
In total darkness down below.
But, "Faster, faster," cried the worm
Escaping from that furry form.

AN ANGRY PIG

A pig he is contented
With the order of porcine.
But how his eyes with anger blaze
When called a dirty swine.

THE BUMBLE BEE

To me it is a mysterie,
That the heavy bumble bee,
Has got such flimsy wings
And still can flee.

THE LADYBIRD

To me it seems quite absurd,
To call a young lady a smashing bird,
And when I think and think again,
To call a bug a ladybird is quite insane.

THE MAGGOT

The maggot wends his loathsome way,
Across some putrid meat.
He has to wend his way because,
The maggot has no feet.

THE HUMBLE TOAD

Ponder friends, the humble toad,
Shrinking deep in dark abode.
But you would shrink were you a toad
And had his eyes and warts b'goad.

A DOG

It's hard at times just to scold a dog,
Though it's tempting for tae belt it.
When it's ate your ice-cream cone
And the ice-cream's hardly meltit.

A PET BULLDOG

My dog jobbied on the carpet,
But I loved that dog so much,
I hudnae the heart tae scold it,
So I kicked it in the crotch.

A CATERPILLAR

A caterpillar wi' anxious eye,
Watched a fluttering butterfly,
And swore as he ate some juicy leaves
"You'll no' get me up in one of these!"

THE CHIMPANZEES

We're descended from the chimpanzees.
Yet how clever nature's plan.
The apes prefer to haunt the trees,
And not descend as low as man.

THE CAMEL

The camel is clever unlike men.
The camel makes you think,
For the camel can the whole day long,
Survive withoot a drink.

Two

EPITAPHS TO PET DOGS

BUSTER, CHOKED ON A FISH BONE

How proud I was when I taught you
To fetch my bedroom slippers.
If only I had taught you
To avoid the bones in kippers.

RUDI

We miss your bark and wagging tail,
But what I think we miss the most,
Is the careful way you cocked your leg
And aimed it at the bedstead post.

SPOT

Under this stone lies our dog Spot,
Whose only fault he piddled a lot.
A quiet dog and though seldom seen,
We always knew where he had been.

ANOTHER DOG SPOT

He was full of fleas and scratched a lot
But how we loved him our dog Spot.
He was carried away by a strange disease,
Presumably carried by these same fleas.

MACNAB

The angels called you from on high,
To my regret I wonder why,
Although I trained you every day,
You learned to sit but not to stay.

BEN

Gone is the collie we loved so dear
To Heaven's loving care.
But though we've lost our collie,
At least we've gained a chair.

PERCY, A PET DACHSHUND

We remember that day you went walkies,
And disappeared in the snow.
If only your legs had been longer
And your belly not quite so low.

Three

EPITAPHS TO PEOPLE

SAMUEL BROWN FURNITURE REMOVER

We think of you since you removed
To a higher, heavenly dwelling.
We hope that you can read these words.
For you werenae good at spelling.

A PIPER

Here lies John Adams a piper of fame,
On 7th Januar' he left his hame.
The Lord commanded, "Music cease!"
Now his neighbours rest in peace.

IN MEMORY OF A WOMAN'S HUSBAND

You left me with no last farewell,
You left in such a hurry.
I ponder on that fateful day,
You ate my home-made curry.

A FERRY CAPTAIN

You sailed Life's stormy ocean,
And ended on the rocks.
You left behind fond memories
And piles of dirty socks.

VIOLET MURPHY, ACCIDENTALLY STUNG

A precious flower from us has gone,
Though still in memory.
She stooped to pick a bonny flower,
And was picked on by a bee.

A MAIDEN AUNT

We waited eager for her bequests,
As roon' her bed we quietly sat.
Then she whispered these few words,
"Don't forget to feed the cat."

BACHELOR LUMBERJACK

If only he had run one way
And the tree had fell the other.
The unfortunate Sam MacAdams
Would still be with his mother.

THOMAS BROWN, A FARMER

Choice runner beans, the last he ate,
Ere he stood at Heaven's Gate.
Life is not as it sometimes seems,
Poor Thomas gone but full of beans.

JAMES GRANT, ELECTRIC METER INSPECTOR

I am at home in Heaven, dear ones,
Oh so happy and so bright.
For there's no need to read the meter
In this everlasting light.

BEN GREEN

Ben Green died from a leaking bladder,
He saw a specialist but just got badder
Now through parching summers hot
A fountain springs from this very spot.

A SHOP STEWARD

I think of you today, brother,
But then that's nothing new.
I thought about you yesterday
And the pound you owed me, too.

A MASTER BAKER

A pie fell on baker Thomas Lee,
And much to his surprise,
He found too late, his balding crust
Much thinner than his pies.

A SEAMAN

Here he lies,
Under the ground.
Lost at sea,
And never found.

COWBOY'S EPITAPH

The blow was fatal, even severe,
When he collided with a runaway steer.

A POLITICIAN

A politician of great fame,
He lied with devious skill.
But even though he's gone from us,
Take heed! He's lying still!

A RAILWAY COMMUTER

His last ticket
Took him straight to Heaven.
He wanted a return,
But none was given.

POLO PLAYER

No longer will you mount your mount,
No longer will you gallop.
Since that day you fell aff
And received a fatal wallop.

A FARMER

He ate his lunch,
His last words were few.
"For God's sake, Mary,
Throw away that stew!"

JAMES O'KEEFE

The death knell tolled through the night
It tolled for James O'Keefe,
But his wife it was who told O'Keefe,
For James himself was somewhat deef.

GARAGE MECHANIC

You were towed away from us one day,
How the years have flown!
Now here you lie with sump bone dry,
And all your gaskets blown.

TOM SAMPSON BAKER

He left behind his mixing bowl,
And many heavy hearts.
But not as heavy we're glad to say
As his special home-made tarts.

MASTER MARINER

He sailed the seven seas twice over,
Now here he lies, at last keeled over,
Becalmed beneath a sea of clover.

STEEPLE CHASER

His horse jumped ower a hedge with glee,
But he went through it R.I.P.

LOCAL POACHER DATE UNKNOWN

Tired and weary he avoided fuss,
But not, it seems, a blunderbuss.

JOHN BAKER AND FAMILY

Here lie within these vaults
John Baker and his cousin,
His brothers seven and sisters four,
Complete this Baker's dozen.

EPITAPH TO A PUBLICAN

A publican stood at Heaven's Gate,
Wi' sweat his brow was lacquered.
He said, "I can't take any more,
For I'm completely knackered."

"My friend," St Peter sadly said,
To keep a pub was folly,
Come in and rest your weary head,
You're clearly off your trolley!"

EPITAPH TO AN ELDERLY SPINSTER

A maiden all her life was she,
That's how her life turned out to be.
For love or money she couldn't be bought,
So the worms they got what the men did not.

Four

PEOPLE

A WEE PRAYER

I thanked the Lord for all good things,
Things that I maun treasure.
He said to me as he lookit doon,
"For you it was a pleasure!"

A MEAN WOMAN

The meanest woman I ever met,
Used the budgie's eggs for an omelette.

LOVE IN AN ALPINE POOL

We inhaled the scent of pool-side flowers,
As we splashed barefoot for many hours.
But no Alpine meadow smelled so sweet,
As bonnie Annie's fresh washed feet.

MOONLIGHT LOVERS

We watched strands of cloud aboon,
Trail 'cross the bald and rounded moon.
I kissed my lass and softly said,
"It's no' unlike your Faither's head."

THE FARMER

How quiet the river runs today!
It's bosom swells in ecstasy.
The rolling waters proudly flow,
A cow stands on a farmer's toe.

The years flow on just like the river.
The farmer ponders, "Well I never!"
As he sits by the garden gate
In a shoe size twelve the other eight.

LETTER TO THE EDITOR

Dear Sir,
Never bite your finger nails,
It makes your fingers lumpy.
Never bite your finger nails,
Yours sincerely, Stumpy.

YESTERDAY'S GIRLS

Where are the girls of yesterday?
The bonnie Highland lassies?
They're auld and grey and grannies now,
Half-hidden in moustaches.

GOSSIP

If people were unblemished,
Wi' haloes roon' their heid,
They'd be naebody bad tae talk aboot,
And days gey long indeed.

A CHEERY MAN

"Nae wonder," said the wife,
"Ma man's sae cheery,
Ah've just smelt his breath,
And his breath smells beery."

A GREEDY MAN

A man was eating a sandwich in bed,
"Haw, gie us your crust",
His hungry wife said.
So slyly that greedy man uncovered his head.

PROGRESS

I remember the fields,
Wherein I played as a child.
I went back one day
To find factories there,
And the fields completely spiled.

STRANGE THOUGHTS

Sometimes I have strange thoughts,
And sometimes I havenae ony.
But was it waves or wheaten flour
That immortalised Marconi?

KEEPING UP WITH THE NEWS

A man was stuck in a pillar-box,
Goad, he was nearly roastit,
Says, "I like to keep up wi' the news,
So the missus keeps me postit."

THE FIREMAN

To be a fireman was his desire,
To dowse the flame - pit oot the fire
And rescue ladies in night attire.

But once a boy was loudly wailing,
His heid stuck fast between a railing,
All efforts to save him unavailing.

Then the gallant fireman came
And bent the rail and freed the wean.
And wiped his nose and sent him hame

So, if you would a fireman be,
Here's a hint for you from me.
The moral here, what I suppose is,
Keep hankies handy for wee boys noses.

A WORRIED MOTHER

A boy's Maw was worried,
Said his Paw, "Don't be absurd,
Although it's efter twelve o'clock,
He'll be chatting up some bird."

A KEEN GARDENER

A gardener freen was awfy keen,
Worked day and night wi' his barra,
Caught oot wan night wi' frost and snaw,
Found frozen tae his marra.

THE WEARY HIKER

Pity friends, the weary hiker,
Stumbling through the lonely glen.
Wi' each step he cries oot, "Mammy!"
For he's got blisters, eight or ten.

ANNIVERSARY DINNER

On what shall you dine, my love?
What delights shall pass your lips.
"A hauf, a pint of heavy,
Double porker, egg and chips."

THE PARISH

Greenfly ravished the Parish,
The roses were in decay.
The Minister spoke unto his flock,
"Come Brethren, let us spray."

THE PATRIOT'S SONG

"These are my mountains,"
Is the patriot's song.
But they belong to the landowner,
So the song must be wrong!

FAMILY LIFE

The washing hung steaming by the fire,
A pot was bubbling full of stew.
A man sat heavy on a chair,
For he was stewed and steaming too.

MARRIED COUPLE

We quarrelled violent yesterday,
My spouse struck me on the mouth.
Although we made it up again,
I thtill think my thpouth a louth.

A POOR BOY

A boy came running home one day,
Says, "Maw, ma knees is skint."
His Maw, looking in her purse,
Says, "Look son, I'm skint, tae."

CHILD'S DOLLY

I have a little dolly,
Wi' sawdust for a brain,
Some fell on the carpet
And Daddy got the blame,
For Mammy had cleaned the carpet
And thought Daddy wis scratching
His heid again.

SAD BOY

A wet-eyed boy stood
At the Chippy's closed door
Haudin' money in his mitts,
"Sonny," Ah said wi' great concern,
"Ah think you've had your chips."

JACK'S MAW

Two boys made fun o' Jack's large Maw,
But Jacky didnae mind at a",
For he had mair Maw
Than the other twa.

A LADY

She says she isnae snobbish,
Though she wears expensive clothes,
Funny though, intit,
How the rain gets intae her nose?

A VAIN YOUNG MAN

"Ah'm no' very fat",
Said the vain young man,
"But if Ah had tae choose
Ah'd rather wash ma face
Than tie ma shoes."

FROGS AND TOADS

Frogs and toads have pimply plooks,
Mothers, fathers, sons and daughters,
But nature shields us from their looks,
By hiding them in murky waters.

ARISTOTLE

Head in hand I try to probe
The profound Aristotle.
Then a voice deflects my thoughts,
"Any wine left in your boattle?"
Is it better, then I think,
To probe the depths of Aristotle,
While my friend with guzzling sound
Probes the depths of my wine boattle?

FUNNY FOLK

Some folk are funny
And some are fickle.
But strange folk are those
Who don't laugh when you tickle.

PIPE BANDS

Every time the pipe bands play,
People can be heard to say,
"Is it true or is it not?"
People are a nosey lot.

SMOKE SIGNALS. A RED INDIAN POEM

A tourist asked an Indian Brave,
About smoke signals in the sky.
"These puffs of smoke from your wigwam,
"What do they signify?"
The Indian took a few deep breaths,
He was from the hunt returning,
"Friend," he said, "It's breakfast time
"And the bliddy toast is burning!"

Five

LIMERICKS

A GIGGLING MAN

A man addicted to giggles,
Wrapped wool around strong, onion piggles
Said he with a smile,
It makes it worth while,
When I swallow a piggle it tiggles!"

A SAILOR

An ex-sailor, submarine,
Went shopping for strawberries and cream.
He said with a smile,
"I've walked many a mile,
But I'm blessed if I know where I've been!"

CONSIDERATE FARMER

A considerate farmer from Bray,
Fed his beasts in a kindly way.
Two goats and a hen,
With a ballpoint pen,
Chose the menu for the very next day.

His children, sad to relate,
Were treated more unfortunate.
They had, to their sorrow,
Steal food, beg or borrow,
For their father didn't care what they ate.

BIRD SONG

An old man woken up each spring
By birds pairing up to sing.
Pulled the tail off a dove,
Who was deeply in love,
And gagged a small wren with its wing.

MACFEE

A careless young man named MacFee,
Chopped down a huge elm tree.
He should have run faster,
Now he's in plaster,
That's the consequence, MacFee you see.

A MISER

A miser from downtown Rangoon,
Drank soup through a hole in a spoon.
Said he with a smile,
It's really worth while,
For the soup I save is a boon.

SCOTTISH CAFE

In a cafe in Scotland so bonnie,
A waiter confessed to his crony,
"We've got plenty Buitoni,
"Some nice macaroni.
"But Haggis we dinnae have ony."

A MALODOROUS MAN

A malodorous man from Belham,
Smelt so bad his friends didn't tell him.
He spent many hours,
Smelling sweet flowers,
It's lucky the flowers couldn't smell him.

A FISHMONGER

A dreadful seaside Fishmonger,
Kept his fish longer and longer,
Till the smell got so bad,
It angered his Dad,
Who flogged him for hours with a Conger

Six

ODDS AND ENDS

FARM PIG

For years they tried to catch him,
But he swore he'd never be taken.
He was twice as fast as the farmer,
Who called him Streaky Bacon.

THREE-LEGGED DONKEY

A donkey wi' his hind leg missing,
Though he wisnae in any great pain.
Fervently hoped the farmer's wife,
Widnae talk tae him again.

FINE WINE

"Red or white wine, Sir?"
Asked the waiter being kind.
"It disnae matter to me," Ah said,
"Because I'm colour blind."

A HARD-BOILED EGG

When you want a hard-boiled egg,
It really isnae funny.
For when you want it hard-boiled,
It always turns oot runny.

AN OUTSIDE BOG

A boy threw petrol doon an ootside bog,
Efter dinner his faither went tae contemplate,
He lit his pipe - boom! - flew skywards,
Roon his neck the toilet sate,
His wife astonished murmured sadly,
"It must have been something that he ate."

THE POOR POET

What pensive streams of thought
Percolate his massive crust,
As he pens his verse upon his papyrus.
And yet his wife
Who vacuums up those piles of discarded paper balls,
Through trembling lips emits a curse,
And turns purple when the bin liner bag is burst.

SPRING BULBS

Under the snow wee bulbs are lying,
They look like onions but are no' for frying.
And when spring skies are vivid blue,
Wee crocus buds come speeding through.

LEADER OF THE BAND

He marched ahead of the cymbal player,
Of danger he was unaware.
A sudden bang from the percussion,
A cry of pain - acute concussion.

MY ISLAND

I long for that island
I ken very weel.
Haunt of the ferret
And of the grey seal.
Nae wunner ma hert's
Aye tugging ma vest
Tae return tae that island
Which I love the best.

I dream of bold mountains
Where red thistles sprout,
Where the stag loups on high
Likewise the brown trout.
And I sit in the doorway
Watching the bees
As they pick their way careful
'Twixt the hairs on my knees.

A CONSIDERATE HUSBAND

A man bought a light weight mower,
Consideration he did not lack.
He was concerned that his loving wife,
Widnae hurt her aching back.

SPRING MORNING

The braw sun is a'shining,
Upon the sprouting corn,
And the hedgehog is a'scratching,
Ere its young are newly born.

There's a sound of heavy thumping,
From a bedroom close nearby,
And the farmer's wife is shouting,
"Get up! Get up! Get up!,
Get up and milk the kye."

Now spring in all its glory,
Its scintillating best,
Calls to everyone,
"Throw away your vest!"

LOVE IN A SUPERMARKET

As I was a'shopping one summer's day,
I met a fair maiden with trolley and tray.
"Where go you, young maiden?" were the words that I
said.
"Kind Sir, to buy dog food and a wee loaf of bread."

My heart pounded madly as I ventured near,
And her blonde hair was blonde,
Except for some dark roots above her left ear.
Now each weekend you'll find us baith haudin' hauns,
Next tae the frankfurters and the big, frozen prawns.

SPRING EVENING

I must away to the fields again,
To inhale the evening breeze,
That blows o'er the short, short grass,
And cows grazing on their knees.

And thence, perhaps, to a country inn,
Enhanced by dandelions in bud,
Where ancient paintings grace the walls
And old men, in rhythm, chew the cud.

CRIME

Killing is a dreadful crime,
Yet in a way I'm guilty too,
Though the only thing I killed
Was time.

IN THE PARK

Now at last it's summertime,
One rejoices in the flowers.
One wonders whence the beer cans came,
One wonders many hours.

THE BLACKBIRD

I watched a caterpillar fall,
From where I sat in treetop tall,
And faintly heard I a squelching sound,
As the poor, little bleeder struck the ground.

PERM

The plainest boy Ah ever saw,
His hair hung doon like midden straw.
He was awfy cheeky and sometimes surly,
But noo he's sweet 'cause his perm's so curly.

COCK CANARY

Wance Ah had a cock canary,
It sung a' day sae lood and clear.
Then it laid an egg wan morning.
Funny bird was it no' queer?

POET'S HEART

The poet's heart it palpitates
Within the poet's chest.
But it cannae palpitate so much
If he wears a dirty vest.

MONEY

Money talks, so they say,
I hear this with a sigh.
For the only words it says to me,
Is simply just good-bye.

AN UNFORTUNATE BOY

A road roller run ower a boy,
"Take me hame," he cried, "For Ah'm sore."
His Maw wis oot when we got there,
So we slid him under the door.

IN PRAISE OF THE HORSE

Oh proud horse and even prouder mare,
No animal to you can compare.
You have such gracious lines when you run,
And your flying fetlocks shake the very grun'.

CHILDHOOD

Is it really true to say,
That only once I passed this way?
A child's world that once I knew,
Of purple thistles webbed in dew,
Of birds and butterflies.
Each single day a Paradise.
Surely there were other things,
Like home work and cruel nettle stings?

FULL CIRCLE

The snail crawls on the cabbage leaf,
The maggot crawls on putrid beef.
The wasp crawls on the fallen pear,
The drunk man crawls in circles on the flair.

SPRING FLOOD AT THE FARM

Begone ye fickle primrose,
False promises ye hae brung,
The rain has poured since early May,
The thrush has not yet sung.
My heart has not yet risen,
Likewise the baker's dough,
And folk are moochin' roon' aboot,
As crabbit as a crow.

The happy smile of yesterday,
Has gone like last year's moon,
And if the rain continues,
The mowdies will a' droon.
The farmyard midden's noo awash,
Away the hens are floating,
The coos are swimming in the byre
And still the rain comes stoating.

Of Mother Nature I despair,
There's times that I could curse her,
For still the rains come drenching down
And things are getting worser.
But hark! there's silence all around
And no incessant drumming,
Bedraggled birds are preening coats,
They feel the sun is coming.

Around the farm upon barbed wire,
Sodden socks are steaming
As darting from behind low clouds
The joyful sun is beaming.
The mowdie's moistened snout appears,
A'thrusting through dead leaves,
His spade-like paws work overtime,
Dispatching hungry fleas.

There's happiness throughout the land
And peace reigns in the byre.
A warm breeze stirs the sleeping bees,
The socks blow on the wire.
Yet dark despair pervades the air,
Sheep faint while sniffing socks,
Till farmer with a gentle hand
Soothes their trembling hocks.

Now Mother Nature bounds around
Her leafy arms outflung,
Spreading green upon the ground
Like the farmer spreading dung.
The auld wife dozes by the fire,
Toasting her carpet slippers.
The collie licks his dripping jaws,
Then eats the farmer's kippers

So ponder on this homely scene,
As you eat and watch the box,
Appreciate your bread and butter
And the farmer minus socks.

BRING BACK THE BANGERS

Oh where is the banger fae yesterday,
Wi' its delicious edible skin,
Wi' the aroma that drifted four hooses away,
When the family got tore in.
Oh where is the banger fae yesterday
That spat fae the pan at me,
And nae sound wis heard but the champing of jaws
When we had them for oor tea.

Oh where is the pie that gladdened the eye
And delighted the human nose,
It's gone wi' the mince, it's long gone since.
And where to no one knows.
Oh bring back the pie that gladdened the eye
Wi' the gravy that dripped doon yer chin,
It congealed there till you could eat nae mair,
Then you sooked it a' the way in.

Oh where is the scone tae pit jam upon,
That held a big daud or mair,
The wans ye get noo don't haud much at a',
And the jam splatters doon on the flair
But where's the big bangers a' bent like bananas?
The wans ye get noo are deid straight,
They taste like broon breid and ye just lose the heid
When they skite right aff the plate.

Ah'll end ma wee rhyme, Ah've no' got much time,
'Cos Ah'm sharing ma toast wi' a moose,
Ah've trained the wee soul tae beg wi' a bowl

And bring back the grub tae the hoose.
There's only wan moose that's loose in ma hoose,
There wisnae enough grub for the rest,
They went wi' their cases, wi' tears on their faces
And their ribs sticking oot o' their vest.

THE DEWDROP

How pretty is the dewdrop
When it hangs upon the rose.
How come it's not so pretty,
When it hangs upon your nose.

THE ZOO

I wandered down to the Zoo today,
To watch the wart-hogs at their play.
An ugly one had a large carbuncle,
Which reminded me of someone's Uncle.

DEEP DESPAIR

Sometimes I swear,
In deep despair,
When I hear the expression,
"It must be somewhere!"

Seven

SLIGHTLY LONGER POEMS

WOODLAND HELL

Near where the nodding bluebell grows,
Atween the beech's wooden toes,
Where foxes sniff and badgers prowl
Beneath the haunt of howling owl.
Where puddocks loup the hale day lang
And trees resound wi' cheerful sang
And horse goes neighing up the hill
After he has drunk his fill.

That's where my boots, approx. size ten
Take me to my woodland den.
Where chaffinch high above is singing
And bluebells wet wi' dew are hinging.
'Tis then when I can go no furder,
(My blistered feet are screaming murder).
Steaming boots are cast aside
And sweat and snails through eyelets glide.

By midge and muse I lie demented,
Fermenting feet by flies tormented,
Face a' lumps by stinging midges,
Ye widnae credit it, wid yez!

That's why, to date, there's just one Bard,
For a poet's life is very hard.

A DAY IN THE LIFE OF A BYGONE POET N'THAT

He wanders alone astride his horse,
Amang leafy woods, amang the wet moss.
He wanders alone 'neath shady bowers,
Counting the days likewise the wild flowers.
He espies a pool and leaps down from the saddle,
Takes off his socks and has a wee paddle,
While admiring the fern and other types of greenery,
All enhancing the pretty scenery,
Which surrounds the pool on all sides,
And through which the speckled trout glides.

Refreshed the poet rests his head upon a grassy sod,
And is quickly into the Land of Nod.
His cares and woes are soon forgotten,
Likewise his false friends who have been rotten.
Meanwhile his horse drinks water through large,
yellow teeth,
While watching tadpoles swim beneath.

An hour later the yawning poet thinks,
"I'm all the better for those forty winks."
And leads his mare and when they fresh grass
encounter,
Lets her eat her fill and then proceeds to mount her.
He gallops hame, with thoughts of fish and chips,
Silhouetted against the sun as it downwards dips.

THE NOODLE SOUP SONG

Noodle soup I love your taste,
Hence this wee praising sonnet.
I love your steaming surface,
With croutons floating on it.

Oh to stir up your delights,
And free your subtle fragrance,
That brings crows flocking round the door,
And other feathered vagrants.

But whiles I dread the noodles,
For there's a lang hair on my chin,
And sometimes quite in error
I sook that long hair in.

I love to pluck the noodles
That cling to my moustache,
And throw them to the sparrows,
With a flourish of panache.

And when I've downed my final bowl,
And drunk my last carafe,
I hope they'll have kind words for me
And inscribe my epitaph.

"Here lies a much-loved man,
His heart was big as a marra,
He loved all his fellow men
And shared noodles with a sparra."

SPRING COMES TO MACHRIHENISH

The blackbird warbles from the highest bough,
Proclaiming that Spring is here, in MACHRIHENISH
now.
While translucent snowdrops far below
Diffuse with light old patches of grubby snow.

And bluetits break the quiet morning's spell
By cheerfully pecking each turning, twisting peanut
shell.
And each morning a lady born in MACHRIHENISH
Seeks with titbits her bird-table to replenish,
Politely noting that it requires another coat of high
gloss vernish.
She also fills half coconuts with hot suet, oats and
mince,
Then after her own breakfast gives her false teeth a
rinse.
But all this noise of whistling, pecking, plus a barking
dog
Disturbs a garden resident - a slumbering hedgehog.

Enraged, this red-eyed ball of fearsome spikes,
Espies a hole in the lady's slipper, then he strikes.
She hopeless tries, this sweet and kindly soul,
To strike the hedgehog with a greasy soup-bowl.

The lady hobbles painful through the soiled snow,
The snarling hedgehog clinging to her toe.
At last she grabs the hedgehog in her mittened haun'
And dashes the culprit to the frozen lawn.

"How like humans", reflects the lady in
MACHRIHENISH shawl,
"These creatures are like humans - you cannot please
them all!"

AND A RATHER DEEP POEM
ENTITLED LOW CLOUDS

Above the dripping dandelions,
Long, low clouds like sausages floated
But they were full of moisture not mince.
I have not seen such long, low clouds since.

GLASGOW NECROPOLIS

Oh just to see such magnificent grandeur,
Reaching with stony fingers for the sky,
If one couldn't control oneself,
It would surely make one cry.
But this presents a danger to the wee birds,
For like when they're hungry flying low,
They could entangle their tiny claws
On the pinnacles below.

Perhaps the most striking of these engraved rocks,
Is a fifty-eight foot soaring Doric-column,
In memory of the Calvinistic John Knox
Who beneath his stony beard is still very solemn.
But consider the sculptor of long ago,
Who created such beauty with hefty blows,
Sneezing strongly in his workshop,
As stone dust infiltrates his nose.

And the sculptor's wife shouts, "Tea up!" in vain,
As through the foggy dust she peers,
For, alas, he cannot hear one word,
For the dust of marble lies thickly in his ears.
In his silent world he works with loving care,
As the muffled female voice attempts to scold,
But the sculptor so engrossed in work is he
That, like his marble, his tea awaits stone cold.

Past monument, pinnacle and spire,
The weary bearers stumble on uneven way,
To halt with trembling, shaky knees
And lower the deceased unto his bed of clay.
Then friends and relatives depart,
From the departed who lies in sweet repose,
And mourners who are dying too but only for their
tea,
Frequently stop to blow their reddened nose!

So, dear friends, take heed before you too expire,
Visit Glasgow Necropolis, with magnificent tomb and
spire,
You will not be disappointed for it's all one could
desire.

ONE OF THE FAMILY

"You must be one of the family now!"
And she gave her boy friend a hug.
"Why'" he asked and she answered,
"Mum's gied you a chippit mug!"

DER PARTY

Ein poem in GLESGA/DEUTSCH

Das Haus war schon gehoovert
Und die Kinder tief im schlaf,
Der Tisch war voll mit Flaschen
Und soon die Korks were aff.
Oh boy ! We had ein Party,
Es war wirklich really nice,
So viele Leute tanzen,
Und auch die kleine mice.

Eine Frau von achtzig Jahren
War voll mit Doppelkorn,
Sie tanzt mit mostly young men,
Sie tanzt bis early morn.
Wir essen Mettwurst gerne
Und Pumpernickel Brot,
Und Leute uns besuchen,
Said, "Whit a lot you've goat !"

Wie lustig war der Abend
Mit so many people there,
Some happy tanzen roon' aboot,
Some schlaffen oan the flair.
Da kam ein blondes Mädchen,
Die Männer gehen crazy,
Die wollen mit her tanzen,
Aber she war far too lazy.

"Sei stille!" said someone plötzlich,
Es klopft Jemand on the door,
Es sind zwei Glesga Polis',
And they want tae know the score."
Zwei Polis' stood mit grossem boots,
Mit faces hart wie Stein,
"Can ye no' keep yer voices doon,
And go easy oan the wine?"

"Ach, go you weg, you Polis',
Warum komm you anyway here,
Wir haben ein great Party,
Und wir trinken Lager Beer."
"Please, ruhig," said the Polis',
You making too viel krach,
You making all street lights go out,
You keeping Leute wach."

Und when the Polis' went away,
Mit their grossem Polis' feet,
We were a wee bit quieter,
Mit plenty things to eat.
Mit Sauerkraut und Würstchen,
Und the best von Rheinland Wein,
You bet we had a party,
We had a high old time.

Endlich kam der Morgen Stund',
Die Leute gehen nach Haus,
Except for one wee kleines Tier,
Ein kleines tanzen Maus.
Das wee Maus war happy,
Und kept springen hoch und hoch,
He tried in vain nach Hause to gehen
But immer missed der Loch.

Oh, Kinders, wenn Ich denke,
Tears kommen in mein eyes,
Wie wunderschön der Party,
Wie lecker die mince pies.
Und Kinders wenn Ich denke,
Of that time so far away.
I forget mein legs are shaky
Und mein Haar so furchtbar grey.

THE BEACH PICNIC

We had a picnic on the beach,
The sandwiches we could choose with ease,
For choice was limited to each one,
Sand on ham or sand on cheese.

TEMPUS FUGIT!
(BEWARE OF THE MIDGES!)

Cause and effect of the opening of Paisley's first
Technical School.

By the banks of the Cart where hogweed brims over,
I was lying knee-deep in a sweet field of clover.
As I lingered awhile in poetical mood,
Watching wee ducks, some naked, some nude,
There suddenly arose a wind of gale force,
Which could easily have couped a big Clydesdale
horse.
And I pondered on each thundering wave,
Why one side convex the other concave?

And I thought to myself, my breist full of yearning,
If only I had the schooling and acquired book
learning,
If only I'd listened to what I was tellt,
My wrist widnae be sair from the cruel teacher's belt.
I could have solved this problem, this problem so
grave,
Why one side convex, the other concave?

And I wondered why the views of this ex-college
town,
Were better by far when one's looking down?

For if you stand on top of Glennifer Braes,
You can see women in Paisley hinging oot claes.
These questions unanswered I went hame tae ask
granny,
And whit she related was really uncanny.

And I listened to granny, who was nobody's fool,
Recalling the opening of the first technical school.
In her day Paisley toon was respected world-wide,
Even beyond the boundaries of Cart and of Clyde,
For the world's troosers were held up by strong Paisley
threid,
Only lowered to half-mast for Shanks of Baurheid.

Though Paisley was famed for both weavers and
bleachers,
It had a grave shortage of eager, young teachers.
Education was poor for a toon built on a bobbin,
Causing complaints from the punters and much
sighing and sobbin'.
Noo at that time the high heid yins often would drool,
At the thought of opening a technical school.

For, let's face it, the weans were a bit dim upstairs,
Capable only of reciting their prayers.
Though maist could read and the clever ones rhyme,
Few Paisley weans could tell the right time.
So the high heid yins agreed on stones fae a quarry,
And when it was finished the men werenae sorry.

The front of the building was best scabbled ashlar,
And folk came to admire it from near and afar.
In November 1900 this magnificent stone pile,
Was officially opened by the Duke of Argyll.
The Duke was impressed and came suitably dressed,
Wearing a clean shirt and a much cleaner vest.

Well, that is the story as tellt by my granny,
Noo up to date wi' her computer and tranni.
That is the story of how the Buddies got learning,
Reflected by their weans who are now more
discerning.
Yet the puzzle remains for the staff maist perplexing,
Why one side concave the other convexing?

So tae find oot the truth aboot waves in a squall,
Gran in her wet suit dived from the toon hall.
But sadly her findings were alas, never found,
Likewise poor granny, believed to be drowned.
Who was last seen aff Largs on the crest of a wave,
Wi' wan side convex the other concave.

THE CHURCH

You can go to Church on Sunday,
But sadly comes the rub.
For you'll hear the name of Jesus
More often in a pub.

THE DOG WHO SAVED CHRISTMAS

You'll have heard many times several wee rhymes
Concerning Greyfriars Boaby.
By his master's grave he stayed true and brave,
Except when he went for a joaby.
But there's another brave hound now asleep in the
ground,
Who helped on a Christmas Eve.
On this night withoot snaw he scratched his heid wi' a
paw,
And this you've got tae believe.

For Santa was stranded his big sledge abanded,
"Cause the AA failed to appear.
A drunk man said, "Hay, want a push wi' yer sleigh,
Or a kick start on wan of yer deer?"
In his fur-trimmed red suit wi' a face like beetroot,
For he blushed like a publican's till,
Poor Santa sat there in deepest despair,
Withoot the dug he'd be sitting there still.

There being nae snaw he was near up the wa',
As he pictured a poor, toyless wean.
Then a stray dug crept near wi' a brilliant idea,
To get the sledge going again.
Soon ower the toon came the sound of Monsoon,
As that dog piddled like mad.
And each moonbeam lit up rising steam,
And Santa wisnae hauf glad.

For a cauld, frosty breeze caused the hale street tae
freeze.
Soon Santa wis on his way,
Wi' his big bag of toys for wee girls and boys,
Who waited for presents next day.
Parents erected a stone resembling a bone,
The sculptor used a ten foot ladder.
Noo each Christmas Day the children stop play,
And lay a wreath in the shape of a bladder.

POOR COW

A coo jumped ower a barbed-wire fence,
And it gave a funny shudder.
The farmer milked his coos that night,
Except one minus udder.

A HOLIDAY WARNING

A wumman when on holiday,
(A wumman no longer young),
Was treated by a doctor,
For sunburn on the tongue.

THE FAMOUS RIVER CLYDE

Chorus:
The Clyde, the Clyde, the famous Clyde
Whose banks are high on either side,
To keep folk oot and the watter inside.

As I sat on the river bank,
My mind was all a'quiver.
What could I write, what should I write,
About this famous river?

I cudgelled my brains to coin a phrase,
What could I write about its famous waves?
As they toppled first one way and then the other,
Threatening to engulf a wee duck and its mother.

I searched my jacket for a pencil stub,
Which was lodged between a jam sandwich and some
other grub.
Carefully I licked the jam from the sharpened lead,
As pure poetry simply poured from my head.

The tide comes up sometimes twice a day,
Bringing fishes upon which big cormorants prey,
And after they've eaten they sit each on a post,
And the fattest wan there has eaten the most.

The Clyde, the Clyde, the famous Clyde,
Whose middle is equidistant from either side.
The tide goes oot and then back in,
Which must be like an elevator to the fish therein.

Now gulls are asleep on thy darkening breast,
Some facing East, some facing West.
Night draws its curtain o'er the quiet river,
And some gulls that are cauld gie a wee shiver.

The river's remarkable, a beautiful sight,
Whether viewed in the rain, in the dark or at night.
Noo thanks to good planning the Clyde's purified,
So take a bath first if you plan suicide.

THE RERR WEE PUB

Ah ken a rerr wee pub
And it's no' sae faur fae here,
Where they use mince pies for ash trays
And they watter doon the beer.
Mine Host is awfy jolly
When he sees you on the batter,
For when he fills your pint wi' slops
He knows it disnae matter.

And when you ask him for a hauf,
A glint comes in his e'e,
For if it's efter nine o'clock
The whisky's just cauld tea.
His merry wife is just the same,
She's here tae dae your bidding.
But when you ask her for your change,
She says, "Aw hey, you're kidding!"

This rerr wee pub is fu' at night,
The attraction is the daughter.
The way she wobbles up and doon,
The boys think she's a stoater.
The punters like the bottled beer,
For the beer is on the flair,
And when that lassie bends right doon,
It's, "Aw, gie us two beers mair."

When she stretches tae the gantry,
The place resounds wi' sighs,
For the pub is jammed wi' punters
Staring at her thighs.
Auld married men, their eyes aflame,
Their merriage vows forgoat,
Make strange noises as they clutch the bar
And mumble in their throat.

Mine Host will serve you sandwiches,
Though there isnae much tae choose,
But wan wee man he thinks they're great
As insoles for his shoes.
A punter ordered sandwiches,
Then he simply lost the heid,
He swore that the landlord's wife
Used her curlers on the breid.

That rerr wee pub's still gaun strong,
Unlike it's wattery beer,
So Ah'll end up wi' a warning
And Ah hope it's crystal clear.
Don't go too early tae that wee pub,
You'll catch the barman by surprise,
Steam ironing the sandwiches
And dusting doon the pies.

A DOG'S LIFE

Life is but a dog's desire,
To sleep all day and then expire.

SPECTACLES

Spectacles are very handy
When you're drinking tea,
For they stop the teaspoon
Fae poking in your e'e.

THE SKYLARK
(A NOSTALGIC LOOK BACK)

Hark, hark, the joyous lark,
That sings o'er hill and furrow,
Entrancing man and beast alike
And tempting rabbit from his burrow.

A sweeter sound that ne'er was heard,
On earth or any other planet,
Enthrals the wondering country child,
As he chews a pomegranate.

The ploughman in his tartan trews
And somewhat dirty vest,
Is lifted from his humble toil
As he this song ingests.

He seeks to hide his feelings,
By tying up his lace,
Then he straightens up to Heaven,
And the sun dries his tear-stained face.

Then comes a call that drowns the song,
"Edgar, your tea is ready!".
The humble ploughman lumbers off,
Emotionally unsteady.

And when he reaches his cottage small,
He holds on to the table.
And sinks down on a wooden chair,
Mentally unstable.

His wife draws something from a pot
And throws it on a plate.
And he says, "Is that all you've got?
Because it's bliddy great!"

He smokes the last pipe of the day,
Then empties it with measured knocks,
Afterwards he contemplates,
Toes peeping from his sweaty socks.

Then tucking up each child in bed,
He ruffles up each sleepy head,
Then gazes at his soiled toes,
As tears gush down his reddened nose.

So, town dweller ere too late,
Point both your ears at Heaven's Gate,
There you'll hear the lark's glad cries
And you'll die happy - a happy demise.

MA AIN WEE DUG

Ah had a notion for a nice wee dug,
And the man he said tae me,
"You'll be aufy pleased wi' this wee dug
Wi' it's original pedigree."

Well, Ah wis proud o' ma ain wee dug
And, although it wis only wee,
Other dugs were jealous
For, boy! that dug could pee.

Aye, that wee dug could cock its lug,
But it cocked its leg forbye,
And people hearing a splashing sound
Stared anxious at the sky.

Ah took it tae the training school
Tae learn tae sit and beg,
But Ah wis fair embarrassed
When it piddled doon ma leg.

Ah took it oan a bus wan night
And it jobbied oan the flair,
And when the clippie saw the mess
She threw a drunk man doon the stair.

But noo ma dug is big and strong
And can fetch and sit and lie,
And when he looks at me yon wey,
A tear comes in ma eye.

Gey lonely wis ma life before,
But noo ma day's complete,
When Ah settle in ma chair at night
And he stretches at ma feet.

SUSIE IN THE SUPERMART

Ah had tae go tae the supermart
Tae buy some table jellies,
The rain it wis jist pelting doon
As Ah pulled oan ma wellies.
Ah went in tae the supermart
And tried tae grab a trolley.
A lady, most indignant,
Poked me wi' her brolly.

At last we had a trolley each
And between the shelves we went,
But that lady wis a reckless driver
And ma ham and eggs got bent.
We crashed intae a counter
Wi' spices a' in rows.
There wis various types of curry
And maist went up ma nose.

Ah fell upon a frozen cod,
It gave a frozen stare,
Ah had fish fingers in ma wellies
And corn flakes in ma hair.
Ah sat and shivered sadly,
In fact Ah felt an icicle
Forming on that part of me
Ah use upon ma bicycle.

The manager he came striding up
And as he said "Oh my!"
He slid upon a table jelly
And squashed ma custard pie.
He grasped me firmly by the arm-
How Ah wished Ah wisnae there,
Although, mind you, Ah fancied him,
But no' his custard hair.

The young man helped me tae ma feet
He said, "Please be contentit,
Now about your shopping, Ma'am,
In future we'll just send it."
Now wance a week Ah sit on ma own,
Jist staring at the telly,
Waiting for ma ham and eggs,
And, of course, ma table jelly.

THE FITBA' FAN'S DREAM

Ah dreamt Ah died a lingerin' death
Efter three months Pat and Mick.
Ma team had let me doon again,
Nae wonder I was sick.
Ah floated gently upwards
And tears were in my eyes.
A ticket for eternity
Tae that terrace in the skies.

Ah stood upon a fleecy cloud,
Hung ma colours oan that gate,
And Peter he came hurrying oot,
Ah hadnae long tae wait.
"Excuse me, sir," I humbly said,
"I seek an entrance here,"
A supporter widnae talk like this
But it rhymes OK wi' "beer".

"Excuse me, sir," Ah humbly said,
"I seek an entrance here
Ma team have let me doon again
And Ah'm dying for some beer.
Though Ah sometimes skipped inside the grun'
And sometimes forgoat tae pey,
Have mercy oan a fitba' fan
For Ah wid like tae stey."

St Peter took an aerosol
And sprayed a gentle breeze,
"Stey faur awa' fae me." he said.
"Doon oan yer dirty knees,
Ah've a list of a' yer earthly crimes,
They've a' been written doon.
A peety Ah've tae kerry it,
Ah've nae pocket in ma goon."

"A man came here the other day,
He died inside the jile,
At least he had his principles
But you're just simply vile.
He only smashed his wife's heid in
And killed his bairnies, three,
But he never threw a pure white stick
That couped the referee."

"Last week you asked a captain
Fur his mither's marriage line,
And when he blew a kiss at you,
You ca'ed, "Gerraf ya swine!"
And, when your team wis losin',
You completely loast yer heid,
You held a mirror tae the goalie's mooth
Tae see if he wis deid."

St Peter gaithered his goonie up,
"You'll no' be here again,
Whoever heard o' a fitba' fan
Stealin' sweeties fae a wean?"
"Ach, Ah'm afraid you'll have tae go.
Ah'll gie you a free transfer
Tae that fitba' crowd below."

A free transfer tae ma freens below
Wis ma ultimate fate.
Ah hurried tae the fitba' grun'
In case Ah wid be late.
Wi' beer cans doon ma trooser legs
And a smile upon ma face,
Ah'll settle for ma Heaven here-
For the other's no much o' a place.

VINEGAR WARNING

What happens to the vinegar,
When the pickles are all gone?
Do you try to flush the sink
Or kill daisies on the lawn?
But don't be like one wumman
Who timmed it doon the John.
Sadly she got splashed
And burned the skin right aff her haun'.

TRAVEL ON

When the kye graze in the sun
Wi' fat udders near the grun',
And moles swing on them for fun,
Travel on, move along.

When the puddock louping by
Sooks milk fae wayward kye
And plays heidies wi' a fly,
Travel on, move along.

When you hear the hedgehog snore
And his punctured wife's loud roar
In the roots of sycamore,
Travel on, move along.

When your semmit's chowed wi' voles
And your ribs show through the holes
'Cos you've only ett twa rolls,
Travel on, move along.

When the midgies in a swarm
Attack your hairy sporran
And you wish you werenae born,
Travel on, move along.

When wee birds is pecking wheat
Aff their dung-encrusted feet,
A sight tae make you greet,
Travel on, move along.

When the bonnie, croodlin' doo
Sits abin your bilin' stew
And dichts steam fae aff its broo,
Travel on, move along.

When the Polis' cry, "Ya bum,
Your shoes is fu' o' dung
And we cannae staun the hum",
Travel on, move along.

DAWN

Dawn has came, the breathless hush
Is broken by a singing thrush.
Dawn has came and went as well
And parent birds sing in the dell.
They sing to their young one 'cos they're happy
And have no need of a disposable nappy,
For their offspring nicknamed Crappy.

A SAD CASE

A woman passed away quite sudden,
Her friend spoke in a thoughtful mood,
"At least she's been on holiday,
And it done her the world of good."

THE RELUCTANT POET

He trumpets not, his jaws are clenched,
No longer does he bray.
For, like his rotten poetry,
His teeth are in decay.

SOMEBODY'S AUNTIE

She sits alone with her coffee cup,
And a pound of custard creams.
Her nose is buried in romance,
Her heart is lost in dreams.

AUTUMN

The fields are now devoid of hay,
As most of it is carted away,
To lie in barn or farmyard stack,
Until required for Dobbin's rack.

"MAGIC"

In oor pub we find it tragic,
We've got a friend we ca' magic.
He disappears - he's never found,
He shoots the craw when it's his round.

PUB REGULAR AT HIS DOCTOR'S

When I'm in the pub at night,
I get this fear, an awfy fright.
Don't know what you doctors call it,
I get this pain when I take oot ma wallet.

THE CONTENTED GOAT

The contented goat disnae need a loat,
He's content wi' grass fae crannies,
He has nae worry aboot his kids,
For they're watched by unpaid nannies.

BRIDGE OF THIGHS

A bridge I know where ladies go
Is watched by a thousand eyes below.
It came to me as no surprise,
That bridge is known
As the Bridge of Thighs.

VEGETARIANS

Vegetarians may not live longer
By refusing a tasty pork pie,
But one thing we do know for certain,
They're far healthier when they die.

Eight

MORE EPITAPHS

A STONE ERECTED TO A BUS DRIVER (WHEREABOUTS UNKNOWN)

The Gates of Heaven opened wide.
The Angels quickly jumped aside
As he raced past the waiting queue,
Which, after all, was nothing new.

EMMA JONES

Emma Jones was called on high,
Before she finished her Custard Pie.
Her dog howled once in deepest sorrow,
Then ate her pie like there was no tomorrow.

ANOTHER BUS DRIVER

The Angels cried "You've came at last!"
But true to form he ran right past.

A GARDENER'S WIFE NAMED ROSE

She passed away one sunny day,
The Doctor gave his diagnose,
Blockage of Greenfly up her nose.

JOHN SMITH GOURMET

Here lies John Smith
With insides corroded.
He ate four Curry Suppers
And then he exploded.

A BEAT CONSTABLE

A well known constable on his beat,
His last words to his wife were sweet.
"I leave you now without a doubt,
That is all, over and out."

A COFFIN MAKER

You had no time to say good-bye,
No time to kiss your loving kids.
No time to take me in your arms,
No time to close your heavy lids.

BRICKLAYER

Laying bricks was his career,
Thousands he laid from year to year.
Toiling away in a sweaty vest,
Now like his bricks he's laid to rest.

AN INSECT COLLECTOR

He caught his last bug
And was drinking hot toddy,
When the Lord paid a visit
And collected his body.

CAPTAIN OF A TUG OF WAR TEAM

Here lies James Adams,
Once strong as a bull,
But not strong enough
To resist the Lord's pull.

A CIRCUS FIRE-EATER

He was in bed when his mother came,
His last gasp a sheet of flame.
His mother sobbed at his bedstead post,
"How will I cook the Sunday roast?"

JOHN PEPPER

Far below this heavy boulder,
The ashes of John Pepper smoulder.
By name and nature very hot,
Hence no snow upon this spot.

Nine

MORE ODDS AND ENDS

A WEE CANNIBAL

"I don't like my brother",
A wee cannibal said.
"But to please you, dear mother,
I'll eat mushrooms instead."

HENRY MCNAB

How do you know old Henry McNab
Didn't leave much in his will?
Well, the family's yet together
And on friendly terms still.

COMFORT

There's nowt can compare
Tae a cumfy auld chair,
Wan ye can recline in
Wi' a decanter you keep wine in.

FAREWELL

The children now have left their home,
They've left their Maw called Peg.
The mother's jaws are streaked with tears
The father's with dried egg.

THOU

A loaf of bread, a jar of wine and thou,
But if thou and thine would be mine
I reckon I could skip the wine.

RAMBLERS

We wandered ower
The hills and dales.
And as there were
No conveniences there,
We carried plastic pails.

TO A HAGGIS

Oh you big, fat greasy beast,
You're fair blown up with lots of yeast.
Folk stare at you whether gaun or comin'
For you've mair curves than a female wumman.

And when the knife parts your bloated tummy,
Whit a smell comes oot, oh yummy, yummy!
So let's be happy we can guzzle,
Unrestrained by man or muzzle.

THE REPENTANT

He lay at his front door, a drunken beast
Till roused at last by a passing priest.
"Turn around," said he, "Don't be a mug."
So he turned around back to the pub.

SUPERMARKET

This ground where once great woodlands stood,
Is now trod on by the multitude
And his wife as they enter with their brood,
In search of instant or convenience food.

A LADY GOLFER

A woman landed in a bunker,
And this was sure to grieve her.
When she asked her caddy whit tae dae,
But he didnae play golf either.

A PROVERB

Here's a wee proverb,
And this is the truth,
A sock on the foot
Is worth two on the mooth.

MOTHER

We sometimes call her Mum,
We sometimes call her Maw.
And to us there is no other,
But, when we are short of cash,
We always call her mother.

A RECKLESS BOY

A boy was walking on top of a wa',
High on rocks above the sea.
His Maw cried, "If you fa' and break your leg,
Don't come running back to me!"

SCOTLAND'S BEAUTY

I remember Scotland's beauty,
Tall peaks tipped with snow,
But I remember most of all,
The midge or mosquito.

BEN LOMOND

The hills of Arrochar,
Look bonny from afar,
But big Ben Lomond,
Takes some beating in the gloamond.

A SLEEPWALKER

A doctor cured a sleepwalker,
And this is what he said,
"To prevent further sleep walking,
Keep a cycle near your bed."

ENTRANCE TO HEAVEN

Mine eyes have seen the coming of the Lord
As he to me came toward.
"Welcome sunshine," he said to me,
"Whit's this I hear aboot your sair knee?"
"Well Sir," I said, "It wisnae ma cough,
But ma sair knee that finished me off."

SPENT YOUTH

My skull was well thatched
Wi' bonny black hair.
When I was a young man,
A devil-may-care.
But noo I'm a baldy,
It sure makes you think.
For there's mair face to wash,
When I wash in the sink.

JOAN OF ARC

Something's puzzled me,
Nearly all my Life.
Wis Joan of Arc,
Really Noah's wife?

THE PLOUGHMAN

Pubs cater for the hungry,
But sadly comes the crunch.
How come the lowly ploughman
Can't afford the ploughman's lunch?

OLD AGE

I love to watch the green grass grow,
While sitting in my garden,
And thanks to my new hearing aid,
Can hear my arteries harden.

How do you know you're growing old?
Well here's a method that's true.
How do you know you're growing old?
When your nose runs faster than you.

Now dust lies in your wrinkles,
And in bed you read a book.
With toothless gums I bite your ear,
But can sadly only sook.

THOUGHT

How the mind boggerels,
When reading such doggerels!

THE MODEST POET

Ah'm still a modest poet,
Though Ah've become a star,
Ah still like ma modest food,
Totties, mince and caviar.

Ah remember when Ah worked on ferms,
Among the dung, unsung,
And Ah don't forget from scenes like these,
That Ah have modest sprung.

Ah'm still your humble poet
Scribbling verses on ma knee,
Wearing a size ten bunnet
When it used tae be size three.

Ah still have ma simple tastes
And remember ma humble roots,
When Ah lie steaming on the flair
Among Champagne Kerry-oots.

Though some stars get affected
By wealth, success and fame,
Ah'm still the same, poor, modest poet
For it's never chinged me nane.